The Jerwood Prize for Applied Arts 1998: Glass

JERWOOD FOUNDATION

SPW

The Jerwood Prize for
Applied Arts 1998: Glass

Exhibition Dates

10 September to 11 October 1998
Crafts Council Gallery
44a Pentonville Road
London N1 9BY
Telephone 0171 278 7700

Tour Dates

21 October to 22 November 1998
The National Glass Centre
Liberty Way
Sunderland SR6 OGL

ISBN 1 870 145 763

Cover photograph by Sara Morris

Contents

7 Foreword
by Tony Ford and Alan Grieve

8 Introductory Essay
'The Melting Pot'
by Michael Robinson

13 Exhibitors
14 Galia Amsel
16 Lise Autogena
18 Tessa Clegg
20 Keith Cummings
22 Anna Dickinson
24 Diana Hobson
26 Keiko Mukaide
28 David Reekie

30 Credits

Foreword

In 1995, the Jerwood Foundation, in collaboration with the Crafts Council, instituted this country's first major award for the Applied Arts, with a £15,000 prize. In 1995, the prize was won jointly by Peter Chang and Charlotte de Syllas for jewellery, in 1996, by Philip Eglin for ceramics, and in 1997, by Caroline Broadhead for textiles. This year our collaboration celebrates glass. In 1998, the profile of British glass is also raised by the opening of the National Glass Centre in Sunderland, with whom we have been pleased to establish the first UK tour of The Jerwood Applied Arts Exhibition.

Although architectural glass has a long history, studio glass is something of a recent phenomenon. It only became viable in the 1960s when the technology available to industry was successfully scaled down, but it is astonishing to see the progress made since then. This is due both to innovation by individuals and to the success of glass courses at a professional level.

The advances in techniques and in aesthetic, as well as the sheer energy of the sector, became clear from the quality of submissions for this award, and the judges had even more difficult a time than usual in judging across such a varied spectrum – from vessels to sculptural glass, from casting to engraving. Their brief, however, was to select the maker "who had made the most outstanding and innovative contribution to glass over the past five years".

The Crafts Council and the Jerwood Foundation are therefore enormously indebted to our five judges – Charles Hajdamach, Principal Museums Officer, Broadfield Glass Museum; Andrew Brewerton, Dean, School of Art and Design, Wolverhampton University; Jennifer Opie, Deputy Curator, Ceramics and Glass Department, Victoria and Albert Museum; Charlotte Sahl-Madsen, Executive Director, the Glasmuseum, Ebeltoft, Denmark; and Zora Palova, Professor in Glass, Sunderland University.

We believe that when the exhibition is viewed, it will stimulate a great interest aid and enhanced understanding and admiration of the art of glass.

The award will be presented on 15 September 1998 during the exhibition of all eight candidates' work at the Crafts Council Gallery, but whoever wins, may our final thanks go to all the glass makers who submitted their applications back in March.

Tony Ford
Director, Crafts Council

Alan Grieve
Chairman, Jerwood Foundation

The Melting Pot

The studio glass movement in Britain is hardly more than thirty years old, yet already so diverse that pulling it all together under one label is hardly possible, and assessing its progress, success and failures, fraught with difficulty. One thing one can say about it, and use as a starting point, is that it was born in art schools and has continued to grow up in them. What we now recognise as its main features, its traditions, were forged in art schools and still remain its basis and continuing ethos: the exploration of, and experimentation with, materials, techniques and processes regardless of prior historical usage; the abandonment of historical forms and notions of glass design and decoration in favour of personal voyages of discovery and expression, and the pursuit of the sculptural and decorative themes at the expense of the domestic and functional. Glass seen and used, as a medium of personal fulfilment rather than as a material for meeting and fulfiling society's needs.

Many factors contribute to the glass situation in arts schools, one is that most students entering them have no familiarity with glass or its history in the sense that they would have with painting. They have no preconceived notions about directions, limitations, traditional usage or any criteria for judging and assessing them, and their first experience of glass as something to work with happens on course. Secondly, they have a finite period in which to come to terms with the stuff and with whatever they are going to do with it. A few short, hectic years later they must mount a show demonstrating the results of their personal odysseys and findings. They are not examined for their mastery of a traditional craft; it no longer is such, and the people doing the examining are still pursuing that mastery, control and usage themselves. Rather they are expected to present an articulate account of what they have to say for themselves at that stage of their development. For most that is it: the acquisition of a degree, a qualification which will allow them access to careers possibly never again involving the use of glass.

This brief maelstrom of creative activity is where passions are roused by, and commitments made to, something never considered before. Very few of our glass-makers had thought of careers in glass as a medium before entering art school. Why not? Well, where would they have seen it? For most students, glass as an eye-opener, is a revelation vouchsafed by the diploma or degree show of a new crop of graduates. What matter if they never make glass again? If they are good, the contributions made by their show can inspire and contribute to the internal art school traditions, feeding them for the next several years.

It may not be just glass that accomplishes this. Textiles, metal, ceramics, graphics etc. all pour their own particular flavour into that melting pot of influences where would-be artists, designers and craftspeople rub against and look over one another's shoulders. The problem is coming to terms with this new material and all the qualities that one perceives as being natural to it. This difficulty is exacerbated by the fact that the glass that one does see is likely to be in book and magazine illustrations or as 35mm slides blown out of all proportion on a lecture-theatre screen. Such experiences can be visualy exciting, but provide little contact with the material itself, and just become part of all the other incoming stimuli that the student has to clarify and come to terms with.

It is difficult to perceive, let alone establish, any notions of standards and quality in this headlong rush to create. They follow, as personal criteria built upon hard-won experience. The early teachers of glass shared in the experiments of their students more than they taught, and could at best demonstrate the results of their own partial successes in similar ventures, guiding newcomers along the short, barely trodden path to virgin territory. Today, a number of those teachers and artists are living legends, the published and exhibited results of whose experiments have benefited the entire glass movement and accelerated its development.

By the time students reach the end of their brief forced growth, the patterns of experimentation and original research have been well established and form the basis of their methodology, whether in postgraduate studies, private studio work, business ventures or teaching in some other art school. The tradition has been established, and whilst it is a universal phenomenon today, a measure of its success in Britain was demonstrated in "International New Glass", the first exhibition of its kind to be held in Venice in 1996. In the section devoted to work from universities and colleges, Britain dominated, with five institutions out of eighteen from nine different countries showing work by young novitiates.

The dominant trend today is towards casting and other kiln-forming techniques, as is evident in this year's selection for the Jerwood Prize for Applied Arts. The movement itself began in the late 1960s with hot glass, and for a while blowing and a vaguely Art Nouveau/Venetian fashion looked like being its hallmark. However, the self-expressive mode which was asserting itself in all aspects of craft at the expense of older, more historical traditions surfaced in glass to the detriment of blowing, which was already proving to be prohibitively expensive, dangerously subjective and too conformist in its canons, and there was a shift towards more personally rewarding and less restrictive kiln-working methods.

We should not ignore though, the importance of our hot-glass-makers and their ongoing contribution to its development. One of the greatest dangers in all the arts today is the adulation of the fashionable. Impact, first, uninformed impressions seem all important, no matter how facile, gestural, formulaic, or inarticulate they are. Banality, slickness and interactive entertainment seem to be the easiest route to acceptability, and what this has meant in the craft-based mediums is that too often, minor ornamentalists catch the limelight at the expense of genuine artists whose seriousness and commitment is beyond the grasp of mere fashion.

There is a great deal of exciting new activity among young glass-makers, but the most resonant, the richest, and the most articulate work is that coming from the 'older' end, a generation still only in its forties and fifties, whose control and skill is founded in long, arduous practice. And many of these people work in hot glass. Just two of many examples that could be cited: Neil Wilkin, whose mastery allows him not just to produce his own visions but to give form and substance to those of other glass workers; Steven Newell's recent collaboration with Carol McNichol, a wholly original and beautiful, eccentric ceramicist, to produce a series of unique pieces. They may have originated in McNichol's ceramic perceptions, but came out entirely and excitingly glass because of a hot-glass maker's control and interpretive skills.

Another direction now offering great scope is surface decoration. Disdainfully rejected by early blowers as anachronistic and irrelevant, it has seen its own craft revival. Older traditions, such as diamond point and wheel engraving, are still practised, frequently in combination with more immediately accessible techniques such as sand blasting. Some of our wheel engravers are among the most internationally familiar of British artists in glass, and Clare Henshaw is one of the most dramatic talents of the past decade.

If surface decoration has not been one of the basic influences in the Art School tradition, that has been because few surface decorators have taught on university courses yet. This could soon change, though, presenting plenty of scope for picture-makers working in and on glass. If this does happen it could be quite a spectacular challenge.

When the studio glass movement began in Britain in the late 60's, the art/craft argument was in full swing. Today, in 1998, areas such as glass, once dismissed as 'craft', are so strong, vigorous and independent that they can address the debate without reference to any other activity. It is possible to talk about the arts of the glass-maker, phenomena that constantly surprise us, but is it possible to talk about glass as art? About statements in the medium of such strength and content that they transcend the beautifully decorative and ornamental?

Yes it is. The Czechs proved that. In a socio-political situation where creative activities, which did not meet a repressive, authoritarian regime's demands or approval were discouraged if not banned; where freedom of expression was not an option; where developments in Western art were seen as decadent and intolerable and any imagery considered critical of, or antagonistic to, official policy was suppressed, glass became a very powerful and articulate language of personal identity. From the mid-1950s in Czechoslovakia, glass achieved a recognisable national style that continued strong traditions, earned valuable esteem and generated Western currency. For these reasons it was encouraged as a successful socialist venture. Artists, the products of the most effective specialised glass schools and academies in the world, were conscripted into designing for factory production of the decorative and the functional, and into creating architectural works on a scale beyond anything we have yet attempted. To all intents and purposes this was a grand and astonishing feat of communist management and socialist aspirations, but it gave Czech artists the opportunity for making works of discrete yet profound intensity. There could be none of the egocentric, assertive flamboyancy of Western art, yet when we look now at what they were doing in the '60s, '70s and '80s, Czech glass comes across as being sculpturally as powerful and meaningful as anything happening in the media used by Western sculptors.

Glass is an artist's medium, anyone familiar with Czech glass knows that. The question is, have we produced anything yet that compares with it or is heading in that direction? I think the answer is yes, but infrequently. We are still coming to terms with it, with a material and a language that we have never accorded the status that the Czechs do, so that it is still struggling to assert its credibility; to attract enough strong artistic personalities into using it and larger audiences into listening to it. It has always been the stuff that ornaments are made of: beautiful, surprising even, but not particularly challenging. We enjoy stylish refinements and virtuoso performance, but expect strong statement and metaphor to come from other media. This could be why some artists such as Clifford Rainey, not wishing to abandon glass, leave Britain to work in more hospitable environments and others abandon glass for more conventionally acceptable media. The loss is ours.

If there is a disappointing gap, a weakness in the movement, it is the lack of attention devoted to the functional. Despite the superb pieces by Simon Moore and others, it is as if on a scale of merits art is at the top and the functional at the bottom: as if the outdated bigotry "If you can use it, it can't be art" was still given any credibility. It is a very challenging discipline; the production of a completely usable piece of sculpture that expresses all the wonderful qualities of materials used and the excitement of processes and skills stretched. Maybe too much of a challenge. But one must ask, and as users we have the right to, art makers not taking the soft option by going for self expression each time, with its inherent risks of self indulgence, when too few seem to be facing up to the social responsibility of producing beautiful objects for our everyday lives. Never before in history has there been so much art activity in glass, and never before in history have so many of us been forced to put up with such banality and ugliness from factories and fashionmongers.

Glass is healthy enough. The problems lie in our perceptions of it as a medium and our treatment of its users. In 1996, Diana Hobson held an exhibition "Language of Light" in Ireland's prestigious Butler Gallery in Kilkenny. There was no patronising condescension 'artist in glass' as opposed to just artist or sculptor. She was one of many English artists shown there including Gillian Ayres, John Bellaney, Bill Woodrow, Richard Long etc., all selected as important contributors to British Art. When is that going to happen here? Our national art galleries now open their doors to works in materials unmentionable not long ago, but, at the first sign of objects or media previously connected with craft those doors slam shut. This may have been understandable in early days of what was purely a "craft revival", but today, when some of our most original artists are working in those media the exclusion is highly prejudicial and condemns them and their work as second class. It is a difficult and sensitive problem but one that does need constant review and the promise of recognition where due.

Too few museums collect and exhibit work by contemporary glass-makers, and whilst there are outstanding exceptions, there is a xenophobic tendency to handle only English glass, giving no indications of its value in world terms. Important exhibitions of international glass are so rare that students wishing to see such must travel at their own expense. Prolonged underfunding of our national institutions has reduced their contemporary glass collections to little more than token holdings, despite the enthusiasm of their staff. We can only hope that the new National Glass Centre in Sunderland will do something to redress this.

The Crafts Council and Contemporary Applied Arts do make great efforts, but with so many areas of activity under their remit, major glass shows are too few. "Contemporary British Glass" was in 1992–1993. How many young artists since then have had the chance to see the best, the competition they must challenge.

If public bodies are so limited in their support, what of the private sector? One can see glass as a craft activity in a number of multimedia commercial galleries, but few can afford, or will risk showing, the topquality work that gives our best artists the reputations they have earned abroad.

This is why Studio Glass Gallery, London is so important, not only as an organiser of shows of British glass to tour abroad, but as the only venue in Britain where top-quality new foreign glass can be seen constantly.

The CVs of our mature glass-artists demonstrate their international standing and importance and we need not worry about the younger ones. Artists are archetypal, they are born with the tenacity, persistence, resilience and remorselessness of vermin, they will outlast our indifference and incomprehension and win the adulation and respect of future generations. But it is sad that we should pour so much of our public and private wealth into the flashier, more easily accessible arts whilst doing so little for people making just as valuable and genuine a contribution to the intellectual, physical, and spiritual quality of our age.

In this light, The Jerwood Prize for Applied Arts, as an open competition and financial reward, is a most significant and prestigious event. It is a celebration of skill and vision and a stimulation and encouragement to both young emerging makers and mature and established figures. By both the accolade it offers, and the controversy it inevitably creates, it is bound to raise levels of debate and criticism as well as production. It is already an important institution in the Applied Arts.

Michael Robinson

Former Curator of Decorative Art,
Ulster Museum, Belfast,
who built the Contemporary European
Collection of Decorative Arts,
now freelance lecturer and writer

The Exhibitors

Galia Amsel
Lise Autogena
Tessa Clegg
Keith Cummings
Anna Dickinson
Diana Hobson
Keiko Mukaide
David Reekie

Galia Amsel

Based in London
Born London, 1967

Education
1989 - 91 Royal College of Art
1986 -89 Middlesex Polytechnic

Selected exhibitions
1997 Clara Scremini Gallery, Paris (solo show)
1996 Venezia Aperto Vetro, Italy
1994 Showcase, Crafts Council at the Victoria and Albert Museum and Contemporary Applied Arts, London
1993 The Glass Show, Crafts Council, London and tour

Major grants/awards/prizes
1994 Shortlisted for Worshipful Company of Glaziers Glass Award
1993 Prince's Youth Business Trust Travel Award
1993 Crafts Council Setting Up Grant

Notable commissions/collections
1997 Lee Valley Regional Parks Authority, Tottenham Marshes
1996 Ulster Museum, Belfast
1995 Association of Business Sponsorship of the Arts Awards
1994 Victoria and Albert Museum Collection

Teaching/lecturing posts
1995-6 University of Sunderland
1993-1995 Visiting Lecturer, Glasgow School of Art, Edinburgh College of Art Staffordshire University, University of Sunderland

My work highlights the unique and opposing characteristics of glass: transparency, fragility, strength and flexibility. I combine many kiln-forming techniques, often stretching their limitations to achieve the appropriate qualities that express my ideas on movement, balance, tension and rhythm, paying attention to detail from model and mould making to applying the final texture and polish. My sensitivity to the material and originality in use of form and process has created challenging and intriguing pieces that work on many levels.

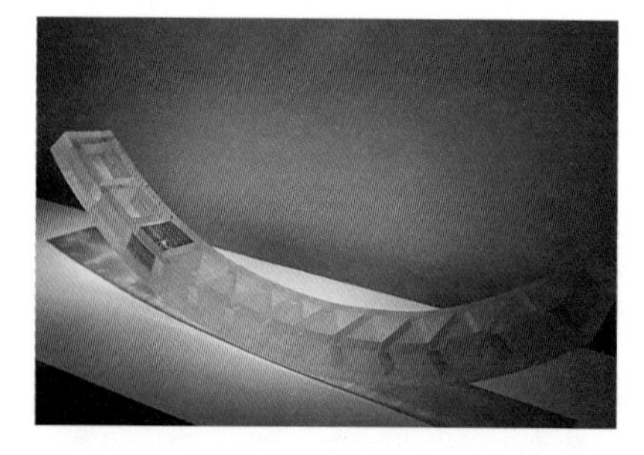

Sequence, 1997
Cast and slumped glass

Right: Seeds 1,2 & 3, 1997
Lost wax, cast glass

Lise Autogena

Based in London
Born Denmark, 1964

Education
1997 Goldsmiths College, University of London (MA Fine Art Curating with Distinction)
1995 Architecture School of University of East London (MA Art in Architecture)
1987-89, '90-'91 West Surrey College of Art & Design, UK (BA Hons Fine Art)

Selected exhibitions
1997 Glass, Light and Space, Crafts Council, London and tour
1997 Young Glass, Ebeltoft Glasmuseum, Denmark
1994 Randers Kunstmuseum, Denmark

Major grants/awards/prizes
1997 The Arts Foundation/The Old Possum's Practical Trust
1996/1991 The Arts Council of Denmark awards

Notable commissions/collections
1998 The new Danish Embassy in Berlin Permanent installation commissioned by The Ministry of Foreign Affairs, Denmark Architects: Nielsen, Nielsen & Nielsen
1998 1 Lombard St, Bank - City of London Computer-generated Project
1996-onwards Lead Artist Birmingham Town Hall Millennium Project
1993 The Browonsky Glass Collection, USA

Teaching/lecturing posts
1998 Fine Art Department, Middlesex University, Visiting Lecturer
1998 Staffordshire University Glass Department, Visiting Lecturer
1998 The Danish Design School, Visiting Lecturer
1995 and 96 Bildwerk Frauenau, Germany

I have spent several years researching perceptions of light involving computer technology for visualisations of how glass can inhabit space. My work in glass has been informed by the changing perceptions introduced by new technology and by the ability of glass to embody light. I have developed large-scale glass sculptures, structures and constructions based on X-rays and the mechanics of the body. This kind of excavating interior spaces has informed my recent work as a Lead Artist for Birmingham Town Hall Millennium Project, involving the idea of casting the exterior building in glass to replace it deep within the building structure.

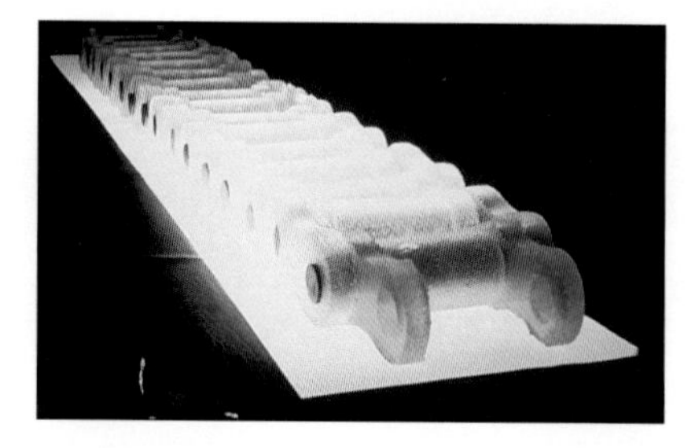

Spine I, 1993
Cast glass elements and metal fittings

Right: Study for Spine VI , 1994
Computer generated moving image of glass object

Tessa Clegg

Based in London,
Born London, 1946

Education
1979-82 Stourbridge College of Art and Technology

Selected exhibitions
1996 Venice Aperto Vetro, Venice, Italy
1996 Clara Scremini Galerie, Paris, France (solo show)
1995 Couleurs & Transparence, Musée National de Céramique, Sèvres, France
1993 The Glass Show, Crafts Council, London and tour

Major grants/awards/prizes
1996, '97 and '98 Corning Museum New Glass Review

Notable commissions/collections
1998 Victoria and Albert Museum, London
1997 Ernsting Foundation Coesfeld Lette, Germany
1997 Musée des Arts Decoratifs, Paris
1997 Corning Glass Museum, New York

Teaching / lecturing posts
1997 Royal College of Art
1992 Middlesex University

In the last five years my work has changed and developed dramatically. In 1993, I was still involved in the concept of timeless beauty. It was the end of a long apprenticeship. I had invented for myself the glass-making process, kiln-formed glass-casting, and was ready to express that mastery. I began to make more sculptural, abstract forms. Minimal and contemporary in concept, they relate to hidden space, colour, transparency, light and shadow, and internal and external volumes. Always vessels, but a play on function and containment.

Red Ring, 1997
Cast glass

Right: Red Bead, 1997
Cast glass, collection Dan Klein

Keith Cummings

Based in Worcestershire
Born London, 1940

Education
1962 Durham University

Selected exhibitions
1997, '98 and '99 International Shoebox Sculpture, Hawaii and 15 US venues
1996 Venezia Aperto Vetro, Museo Correr, Venice
1993/4 The British Glass Show, Crafts Council, London and tour
1993 Visions of Crafts, Highlights from Crafts Council Collection

Notable commissions/collections
1998 Shipley Art Gallery, Gateshead
1997 Birmingham Museum & Art Gallery
1995 Musée des Arts Decoratifs, Paris
1994 Contemporary Art Centre, Schalwick, Netherlands

Teaching / lecturing posts
1993 - present, Professor of Glass Studies, University of Wolverhampton

As a teacher and practitioner since 1962, I have contributed to the development of glass as a creative and educational medium. I have specifically helped establish the kiln-forming of glass as a coherent discipline capable of sustaining high-level craft practice. I have taught at Stourbridge College, the Royal College of Art and latterly at the University of Wolverhampton. Numerous eminent glass artists have been students of mine. I have published books on kiln-forming in 1980 and 1997 that enjoyed worldwide readership.

Sleeper, 1997
Kiln-cast with copper

Right: Tallis, 1996
Kiln-cast with bronze

Anna Dickinson

Based in London
Born London, 1961

Education

1983-85 Royal College of Art
1979-82 Middlesex Polytechnic

Selected exhibitions

1997 Gallery Von Bartha, Basel, Switzerland (solo show)
1996 Venezia Aperto Vetro (guest of honour), Italy
1996 Objects of our Time, Crafts Council, London and tour
1993 Kurokabe Glass Museum, Japan (Solo Show)

Notable commissions/collections

1998 Paul Bedford commissioning piece for Victoria and Albert Museum, London
1997 Musée-Atelier du Verre de Sars-Poteries, France
1997 Leschot Foundation, Switzerland
1993 Kurokabe Museum, Japan

I have worked full time in glass since 1981, and have exhibited in over 30 shows both nationally and internationally. My speciality is electro-formed glass, a technique I have virtually pioneered in this country. Continual research and experimentation in this area is central to my work. I combine many techniques in the production of a piece, all of equal importance to me. Producing only ten to 15 works annually allows me to consider each piece fully, continually striving to achieve perfect balance and harmony. High quality and excellence in both technique and design have always been my priority, and are now synonymous with my work.

Tall black cut vase with blue rim, 1997

Right: Grey cut vase, 1998

Diana Hobson

Currently working on sabbatical in USA
Born Stoke-on-Trent, 1943

Education
1973-76 Royal College of Art (MA, RCA)
1959-64 Stoke-on-Trent School of Art

Selected exhibitions
1997 Via Venice to Ebeltoft, Glasmuseum, Denmark
1996 Venezia Aperto Vetro, Italy
1996 Language of Light, Butler Gallery, Kilkenny Castle, Ireland
1993 The Glass Show, Crafts Council, London and tour

Notable commissions/collections
1997 Victoria and Albert Museum Alistair Pilkington Memorial Fund
1996 Butler Gallery Collection, Kilkenny Castle, Ireland (Serpent from Language of Light)

Teaching / lecturing posts
1993, '95, '97 and '98 Visting Lecturer Royal College of Art
Sept 1997 Inspirational Workshop Leader with Tessa Clegg, Craig Mackay (photographer) and Alan McLeod, Northlands Creative Glass, Lybster, Scotland

My current mixed media work with glass builds on pâte de verre started in 1980, and now developed through teaching workshops. Aesthetic and technical innovations such as matrixing with stone, earth and objets trouvées, have created potential for pâte de verre to reach qualities not seen in glass before. My latest innovations are aesthetic. I aim to reach beyond processes to a refined and minimal conceptual essence.

Talking Stick, 1994
Cast optical glass, bronze

Right: Light Circle detail, 1994
Cast optical glass, bronze

Keiko Mukaide

Based in Edinburgh
Born Tokyo, 1954

Education

1989-91 Royal College of Art
1972-76 Musasino Art University, Tokyo, Japan

Selected exhibitions

1998 Beyond Material, Oriel Mostyn, Wales
1997 Glass Landscape Garden, Manchester City Art Gallery, UK (solo show)
1997 Braggiotti Gallery Amsterdam, Netherlands (solo show)
1995 Musée-Atelier du Verre de Sars-Poteries, France (solo show)

Major grants/awards/prizes

1994, 1996 Award for Individual Development, The Scottish Arts Council
1993 Start-Up Grant, The Scottish Arts Council
1993 The Minister of International Trade and Industry Award, Japan

Notable commissions/collections

1997 Large Hexagonal Wavy Bowl, Crafts Council, London
1995 Shiraniu No 9, Le Portage des Eaux Musée-Atelier du Verre de Sars-Poteries, France
1995 Hexagonal Wavy Bowl, Victoria and Albert Museum, London
1993 Water Edge No2, Kunstmuseum Düsseldorf, Germany

Teaching/lecturing posts

1995 to date, Robert Gordon University, Gray's School of Art, Aberdeen
1993 to date, Artist in Residence, Bink Trust Fellow, Edinburgh College of Art

My intention has, and always will be, to produce high-quality work which is innovative and forward-looking in terms of ideas and experimentation. My palette of glass materials has continued to develop during this period. I continue to reveal the inherent quality of fragility and mass, using cast, fused and blown techniques which exploit the very nature of glass itself. I have ambitious ideas, many of which have concentrated on simplicity and purity, with nature being my major metaphor: water, earth, rock, light with subtle cultural links. Reaching beyond conventional approaches, my recent practice has involved ambitious temporary installations. I have stepped into the field of public art, stretching stereotyped understanding of glass and its possible environment with innovation in this sculpturally biased field.

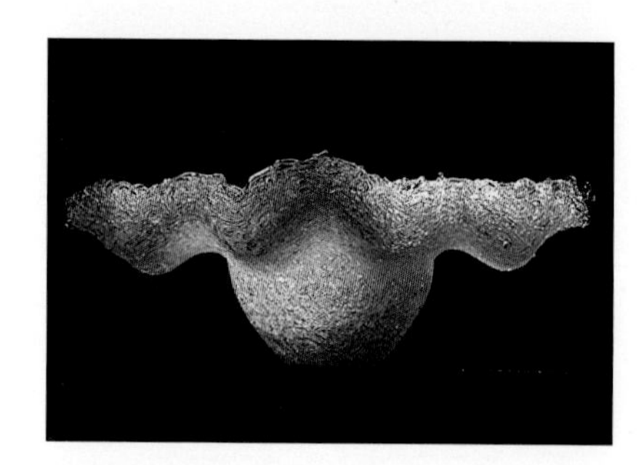

Wavy Bowl (clear), 1994
Fused glass strings

Right: Lucid in the Sky, 1998
Assembled glass fragments, fishing wire, metal frame, detail

David Reekie

Based in Norfolk
Born London, 1947

Education
1967-70 Stourbridge College of Art

Selected exhibitions
1997 SOFA '97, Chicago
1996 Venezia Aperto Vetro, Italy
1995 Miller Gallery, New York, USA (solo show)
1994 World Glass Now '94, Hokkaido Museum of Modern Art, Japan

Notable commissions/collections
1997 Dan Klein, Glass Collection
1995 West Publishing, Minnesota, USA
1992 Victoria and Albert Museum, Collection, London
1991 Crafts Council Collection, London

Teaching / lecturing posts
1994-98 National College of Art, Dublin, Eire
1994 Master Class in Glass, Royal College of Art
1990-93 Pilchuck Glass School, Seattle, USA

Over the last 25 years I have established myself as a highly respected artist exploring and developing techniques in glass-casting and kiln-working, adapting them to my ideas and sculptural work. I have shared my skills through teaching, influencing a generation of young artists. I am committed to closing the gap between glass as a craft and fine art, my work being a continuous development of images, often commenting on the times in which we live. Today I am recognised internationally as one of Britain's leading glass artists pushing the technique of casting into new dimensions.

Balancing Act II, 1995
Lost wax, cast glass, pâte de verrre and found objects

Right: Living in Confined Spaces II, 1998
Lost wax, cast clear lead glass figures on painted wood base

Credits

Photography

Page 14 & 15 *Portrait and work photographed by Galia Amsel*
Page 17 *Computer visualisation with assistance from Joshua Portway.*
Page 19 *David Cripps*
Page 20 & 21 *Work photographed by David Jones*
Page 22 & 23 *Work photographed by Ian Dobbie*
Page 24 *Portrait by Heini Schneebeli, work photographed by Diana Hobson*
Page 25 *Heini Schneebeli*
Page 26 *Portrait by Laurence Winram, work photographed by Keiko Mukaide*
Page 27 *Keiko Mukaide*
Page 28 *Portrait by Duncan Reekie, work photographed by David Reekie*
Page 29 *David Reekie*

Exhibition Organiser Louise Pratt

Catalogue Design Pentagram
Printed by Friary Press, Dorchester

Crafts Council
44a Pentonville Road
London N1 9BY
Telephone 0171 278 7700